LIMITED EDITION

2020

BEST
LENT
EVER®
JOURNAL

WELLSPRING

North Palm Beach, Florida

wellspring

Design by Madeline Harris
Typeset by Ashley Wirfel

ISBN: 978-1-63582-132-1 (softcover)

For more information on this title or other books and CDs available through the Dynamic Catholic Book Program,
please visit www.DynamicCatholic.com.

The Dynamic Catholic Institute
5081 Olympic Blvd • Erlanger • Kentucky • 41018
Phone: 1–859–980–7900
Email: info@DynamicCatholic.com

LIMITED EDITION

Printed in the United States of America

Make This Your

Best Lent Yet.

"Jesus came, saying, 'The time is fulfilled, and the kingdom of God is at hand; repent, and believe in the gospel.'"

– Mark 1:15

DO YOU BELIEVE?

Will this Lent be your best Lent ever?

We think so. That's why we're here. That's why we made this journal for you.

We believe this Lent can be your best Lent ever because we will walk this journey with you. We will guide you, encourage you, inspire you, and pray for you every step of the way. This journal was designed to accompany BEST LENT EVER 2020. If you have not signed up yet, we invite you to do so at BestLentEver.com/2020. You'll receive daily videos that will make your Lenten experience even more impactful.

We made this journal to aid you in the internal renewal and growth we hope will come over the next forty days. Lent is a wonderful season of pause. It is a time of reflection and exploration with God in which he works most mysteriously to give us exactly what we need.

To help you with this time of pause, the journal includes questions meant to provoke thought about your faith life and to provide clarity for where you want to go. You will also find daily readings from *Rediscover the Saints*—the book this program is based on.

We know you have a lot on your plate. This journal is meant to give you just a few minutes every day to connect with God and make the absolute most out of the Lenten journey . . . we believe in the power of baby steps.

We believe God will move powerfully in your life during the next forty days as we journey together.

The question is, what do you believe?

May God bless you and your Lenten journey.

Matthew Kelly

and The Dynamic Catholic Team

WHERE ARE YOU GOING?

It's hard to know if you've made it when you don't know where you want to go. Now's your chance to decide what you want to accomplish this Lent.

Is it a regular prayer routine? Is it more self-discipline in a specific area of your life? Is it better communication in your marriage? Is it more peace?

Now's your chance.

Forty days allow you the time to create a new habit that will help you become the-best-version-of-yourself.

Before we get started, take a few minutes to give yourself some direction.

My personal Lenten Habit will be:

This Lent I want to improve in this way:

I will know I have achieved my goal at the end of the forty days if this is true:

I will hold myself accountable to this person:

Remember, you're not alone. We are here cheering you on, and God's grace is always at our disposal. Through prayer and reception of the sacraments, you are well on your way to accomplishing whatever it is God has placed on your heart this Lent.

"Do not be afraid to dream. Perphaps your fear is of failure. There is no shame in trying to attempt mighty things and failing. The shame is in failing to attempt those things."

– Matthew Kelly

DAY 1 | AUGUSTINE: YOU HAVE A FUTURE

Today's Focus:

God never gives up on us—even if at times we give up on ourselves or give up on him.

Personal Reflection:

Watch today's BLE video (BestLentEver.com/Day1) and write down the one thing that resonates most with you.

_____

_____

_____

_____

_____

_____

What do you believe about your past that is keeping you from your future?

_____

_____

_____

_____

_____

_____

What is God saying to you today?

Recommended Reading:

Rediscover the Saints
  • Chapter 1

Today's Gospel:
  • Matthew 6:1–6, 16–18

DAY 2 | WALTER: THE LOVE OF A FATHER

Today's Focus:

The love of God is a mighty thing.

Personal Reflection:

Watch today's BLE video (BestLentEver.com/Day2) and write down the one thing that resonates most with you.

_____

_____

_____

_____

_____

_____

Have you ever allowed yourself to rest in God's love?

_____

_____

_____

_____

_____

_____

_____

_____

What is God saying to you today?

"We all have different experiences of God and his love, and in each personal experience there are meanings and mysteries that unfold throughout our lives."

Matthew Kelly,
Rediscover the Saints

Recommended Reading:

Rediscover the Saints
   • Chapter 2

Today's Gospel:
   • Luke 9:22-25

DAY 3 | STAFF REFLECTION

Today's Focus:

Amazing Possibilities

Personal Reflection:

Watch today's BLE video (BestLentEver.com/Day3) and write down the one thing that resonates most with you.

How has God opened your heart and mind to new possibilities this week?

What is God saying to you today?

"Can the wedding guests mourn as long as the bridegroom is with them? The days will come when the bridegroom is taken away from them, and then they will fast."

Matthew 9:15

Recommended Reading:

Today's Gospel:
• Matthew 9:14-15

DAY 4 | GOSPEL REFLECTION: THE DESERT

Today's Focus:

Life is a physical and spiritual experience.

Personal Reflection:

Watch today's BLE video (BestLentEver.com/Day4) and write down the one thing that resonates most with you.

_____

_____

_____

_____

_____

_____

In what way is God inviting you to the desert of solitude to evaluate your life?

_____

_____

_____

_____

_____

_____

_____

What is God saying to you today?

Recommended Reading:

Tomorrow's Gospel:
• Matthew 4:1-11

FIRST SUNDAY OF LENT | WEEK IN REVIEW

Today's Focus:

A Week in Review

Personal Reflection:

Watch today's BLE video (BestLentEver.com/FirstSunday) and write down the one thing that resonates most with you.

_____

_____

_____

_____

_____

_____

_____

Looking back on this week, what have you learned about yourself, God, and the world that you hope will change the way you live next week?

_____

_____

_____

_____

_____

_____

What is God saying to you today?

Recommended Reading:

Rediscover the Saints
  • Chapters 1 - 2

DAY 5 | IRENAEUS: FULLY ALIVE

Today's Focus:

God is interested not only in our spiritual activities, but in every aspect of our lives.

Personal Reflection:

Watch today's BLE video (BestLentEver.com/Day5) and write down the one thing that resonates most with you.

_____

_____

_____

_____

_____

_____

When was the last time you felt fully alive?

_____

_____

_____

_____

_____

_____

_____

_____

What is God saying to you today?

Recommended Reading:

Rediscover the Saints
  • Chapter 3
Today's Gospel:
  • Matthew 25:31–46

DAY 6 | BENEDICT: DAILY ROUTINES

Today's Focus:

Few things bring us happiness like deeply rooted daily routines. There is something about healthy routines and rituals that leads the human person to flourish.

Personal Reflection:

Watch today's BLE video (BestLentEver.com/Day6) and write down the one thing that resonates most with you.

_____

_____

_____

_____

_____

_____

_____

Do your daily routines reinvigorate you?

_____

_____

_____

_____

_____

_____

_____

What is God saying to you today?

Recommended Reading:

Rediscover the Saints
• Chapter 4

Today's Gospel:
• Matthew 6:7–15

DAY 7 | TERESA OF AVILA: THE FIRST ROUTINE

Today's Focus:

Nothing will change a person's life like really learning how to pray.

Personal Reflection:

Watch today's BLE video (BestLentEver.com/Day7) and write down the one thing that resonates most with you.

_____

_____

_____

_____

_____

_____

Have you ever been taught how to pray?

_____

_____

_____

_____

_____

_____

_____

_____

What is God saying to you today?

Recommended Reading:

Rediscover the Saints
   • Chapter 5
Today's Gospel:
   • Luke 11:29–32

DAY 8 | IGNATIUS OF LOYOLA: EMOTIONAL INTELLIGENCE

Today's Focus:

If we really want to understand what is happening in the world around us, we first need to explore what is happening within us.

Personal Reflection:

Watch today's BLE video (BestLentEver.com/Day8) and write down the one thing that resonates most with you.

_____

_____

_____

_____

_____

_____

Are you an emotionally intelligent person?

_____

_____

_____

_____

_____

_____

_____

_____

What is God saying to you today?

"The good we do never dies. It lives on forever—in other people, in other places, and in other times."

Matthew Kelly,
Rediscover the Saints

Recommended Reading:

Rediscover the Saints
  • Chapter 6

Today's Gospel:
  • Matthew 7:7–12

DAY 9 | STAFF REFLECTION

Today's Focus:
Amazing Possibilities

Personal Reflection:
Watch today's BLE video (BestLentEver.com/Day9) and write down the one thing that resonates most with you.

_____

_____

_____

_____

_____

_____

_____

How has God opened your heart and mind to new possibilities this week?

_____

_____

_____

_____

_____

_____

_____

_____

What is God saying to you today?

"Go first and be reconciled with your brother, and then come and offer your gift."

Matthew 5:24

Recommended Reading:

Today's Gospel:
• Matthew 5:20-16

DAY 10 | GOSPEL REFLECTION: MOUNTAIN-TOP EXPERIENCE

Today's Focus:

We all have mountain top experiences in life, but we live mostly in the valleys.

Personal Reflection:

Watch today's BLE video (BestLentEver.com/Day10) and write down the one thing that resonates most with you.

_____

_____

_____

_____

_____

_____

Describe one of your own mountaintop experiences.

_____

_____

_____

_____

_____

_____

What is God saying to you today?

"And he was transfigured before them; his face shone like the sun and his clothes became white as light."

Matthew 17:2

Recommended Reading:

Tomorrow's Gospel:
• Matthew 17:1-9

SECOND SUNDAY OF LENT I WEEK IN REVIEW

Today's Focus:

A Week in Review

Personal Reflection:

Watch today's BLE video (BestLentEver.com/SecondSunday) and write down the one thing that resonates most with you.

_____

_____

_____

_____

_____

_____

Looking back on this week, what have you learned about yourself, God, and the world that you hope will change the way you live next week?

_____

_____

_____

_____

_____

What is God saying to you today?

Recommended Reading:

Rediscover the Saints
  • Chapters 3 - 6

DAY 11 | FRANCIS: DISSATISFIED

Today's Focus:

It's time to pay attention to the story you are writing with your life.

Personal Reflection:

Watch today's BLE video (BestLentEver.com/Day11) and write down the one thing that resonates most with you.

_____

_____

_____

_____

_____

_____

_____

What are you dissatisfied with at this time in your life?

_____

_____

_____

_____

_____

_____

_____

_____

_____

What is God saying to you today?

"We all carry the seeds of greatness within us. Sometimes that greatness manifests in extraordinary things, but most of the time the greatness of God manifests in us through ordinary things done with great love."

Matthew Kelly,
Rediscover the Saints

Recommended Reading:

Rediscover the Saints
• Chapter 7
Today's Gospel:
• Luke 6:36–38

DAY 12 | THOMAS MORE: THE GENTLE VOICE WITHIN

Today's Focus:

The saints teach us to live boldly by listening to the gentle voice within.

Personal Reflection:

Watch today's BLE video (BestLentEver.com/Day12) and write down the one thing that resonates most with you.

_____

_____

_____

_____

_____

_____

_____

When was the last time you paused to listen to your conscience before making a decision?

_____

_____

_____

_____

_____

_____

What is God saying to you today?

> "Life has a tendency to slip through our hands like water, unless we live each day, each hour, each moment with great consciousness."

Matthew Kelly,
Rediscover the Saints

Recommended Reading:

Rediscover the Saints
  • Chapter 8

Today's Gospel:
  • Matthew 23: 1-12

DAY 13 | JOHN: FRIENDSHIP

Today's Focus:

It is through our relationship with Jesus that we learn how to be a good friend to others.

Personal Reflection:

Watch today's BLE video (BestLentEver.com/Day13) and write down the one thing that resonates most with you.

_____

_____

_____

_____

_____

_____

Do you allow people to really get to know you?

_____

_____

_____

_____

_____

_____

_____

What is God saying to you today?

Recommended Reading:

Rediscover the Saints
  • Chapter 9

Today's Gospel:
  • Matthew 20:17–28

DAY 14 | MARTHA: OUR LONGING FOR BELONGING

Today's Focus:
We all yearn to belong to a loving community.

Personal Reflection:
Watch today's BLE video (BestLentEver.com/Day14) and write down the one thing that resonates most with you.

Are you part of a vibrant community?

What is God saying to you today?

Recommended Reading:

Rediscover the Saints
 • Chapter 10

Today's Gospel:
 • Luke 16:19–31

DAY 15 | STAFF REFLECTION

Today's Focus:

Amazing Possibilities

Personal Reflection:

Watch today's BLE video (BestLentEver.com/Day15) and write down the one thing that resonates most with you.

How has God opened your heart and mind to new possibilities this week?

What is God saying to you today?

"The stone that the builders rejected has become the cornerstone; by the Lord has this been done, and it is wonderful in our eyes."

Matthew 21.42

Recommended Reading:

Today's Gospel:
  • Matthew 21:33-43, 45-46

DAY 16 | GOSPEL REFLECTION: ENCOUNTERING JESUS

Today's Focus:

Every person who encounters Jesus in the Gospel had a powerful experience.

Personal Reflection:

Watch today's BLE video (BestLentEver.com/Day16) and write down the one thing that resonates most with you.

What are you thirsty for in your life today?

What is God saying to you today?

Recommended Reading:

Tomorrow's Gospel:
• John 4:5-42

THIRD SUNDAY OF LENT I WEEK IN REVIEW

Today's Focus:
A Week in Review

Personal Reflection:
Watch today's BLE video (BestLentEver.com/ThirdSunday) and write down the one thing that resonates most with you.

_____

_____

_____

_____

_____

_____

Looking back on this week, what have you learned about yourself, God, and the world that you hope will change the way you live next week?

_____

_____

_____

_____

_____

_____

What is God saying to you today?

DAY 17 | VINCENT DE PAUL: GOD FEEDS US TO FEED OTHERS

Today's Focus:

Sooner or later we rise or fall to the level of our friendships.

Personal Reflection:

Watch today's BLE video (BestLentEver.com/Day17) and write down the one thing that resonates most with you.

_____

_____

_____

_____

_____

_____

Are your friends helping you become the best-version-of-yourself?

_____

_____

_____

_____

_____

_____

_____

_____

What is God saying to you today?

Recommended Reading:

Rediscover the Saints
 • Chapter 11

Today's Gospel:
 • Luke 4:24-30

DAY 18 | HARRY: WITH YOUR WHOLE HEART

Today's Focus:

Everything is an opportunity to create holy moments, to grow in holiness, and to become a-better-version-of-ourselves.

Personal Reflection:

Watch today's BLE video (BestLentEver.com/Day18) and write down the one thing that resonates most with you.

_____

_____

_____

_____

_____

_____

When was the last time you did something with your whole heart?

_____

_____

_____

_____

_____

_____

_____

What is God saying to you today?

"The saints are there during life's great highs and celebrations, and they are there in those dark moments when life brings us low. They are never far away, and they always bring with them the lesson we need to make the onward journey."

Matthew Kelly,
Rediscover the Saints

Recommended Reading:

Rediscover the Saints
 • Chapter 12
Today's Gospel:
 • Matthew 18:21–35

DAY 19 | JOHN VIANNEY: DISORIENTED

Today's Focus:

We are surrounded by possibilities that only God can see . . . . The danger is that we are so attached to our own plans that we cannot even see his plan.

Personal Reflection:

Watch today's BLE video (BestLentEver.com/Day19) and write down the one thing that resonates most with you.

Are you open to the possibilities that only God can see for you?

What is God saying to you today?

Recommended Reading:

Rediscover the Saints
  • Chapter 13
Today's Gospel:
  • Matthew 5:17–19

DAY 20 | THOMAS: WE ALL HAVE DOUBTS

Today's Focus:

Seeking answers to our personal questions and wrestling with our doubt helps us to build a more robust faith.

Personal Reflection:

Watch today's BLE video (BestLentEver.com/Day20) and write down the one thing that resonates most with you.

_____

_____

_____

_____

_____

_____

_____

Do your doubts unsettle you, or do you see them as an invitation to grow?

_____

_____

_____

_____

_____

_____

What is God saying to you today?

"Authentic faith is going to have to wrestle with doubt from time to time. It's important not to lose sight of the fact that this is natural, normal, and healthy."

Matthew Kelly,
Rediscover the Saints

Recommended Reading:

Rediscover the Saints
• Chapter 14
Today's Gospel:
• Matthew 1:16, 18-21, 24

DAY 21 | STAFF REFLECTION

Today's Focus:

Amazing Possibilities

Personal Reflection:

Watch today's BLE video (BestLentEver.com/Day21) and write down the one thing that resonates most with you.

_____

_____

_____

_____

_____

_____

How has God opened your heart and mind to new possibilities this week?

_____

_____

_____

_____

_____

What is God saying to you today?

"And to love him with all your heart, with all your understanding, with all your strength, and to love your neighbor as yourself is worth more than all burnt offerings and sacrifices."

Mark 12:33

Recommended Reading:

Today's Gospel:
• Mark 12:28–34

DAY 22 | GOSPEL REFLECTION: AWARENESS

Today's Focus:

Jesus is constantly inviting us to become more aware of what is happening within us and around us.

Personal Reflection:

Watch today's BLE video (BestLentEver.com/Day22) and write down the one thing that resonates most with you.

_____

_____

_____

_____

_____

_____

_____

In what way do you need Jesus to cure you of blindness?

_____

_____

_____

_____

_____

_____

What is God saying to you today?

"While I am in the world, I am the light of the world."

John 9:5

Recommended Reading:

Tomorrow's Gospel
 • John 9:1-41

FOURTH SUNDAY OF LENT I WEEK IN REVIEW

Today's Focus:

A Week in Review

Personal Reflection:

Watch today's BLE video (BestLentEver.com/FourthSunday) and write down the one thing that resonates most with you.

_____

_____

_____

_____

_____

_____

_____

Looking back on this week, what have you learned about yourself, God, and the world that you hope will change the way you live next week?

_____

_____

_____

_____

_____

_____

What is God saying to you today?

Recommended Reading:

Rediscover the Saints
  • Chapters 11-14

DAY 23 | BERNARD: IN SEARCH OF EXCELLENCE

Today's Focus:
Change for the better is never easy, but it's always worth it.

Personal Reflection:
Watch today's BLE video (BestLentEver.com/Day23) and write down the one thing that resonates most with you.

_____

_____

_____

_____

_____

_____

Are you committed to the pursuit of excellence?

_____

_____

_____

_____

_____

_____

What is God saying to you today?

Recommended Reading:

Rediscover the Saints
 • Chapter 15

Today's Gospel:
 • John 4:43–54

DAY 24 | THERESE OF LISIEUX: IT'S THE LITTLE THINGS

Today's Focus:

The simplicity of the Gospel is powerful when it is actually lived.

Personal Reflection:

Watch today's BLE video (BestLentEver.com/Day24) and write down the one thing that resonates most with you.

_____

_____

_____

_____

_____

_____

_____

What list of attributes describes your best self?

_____

_____

_____

_____

_____

_____

_____

What is God saying to you today?

Recommended Reading:

Rediscover the Saints
  • Chapter 16

Today's Gospel:
  • John 5:1–16

DAY 25 | MAXIMILAN KOLBE: I WILL TAKE YOUR PLACE

Today's Focus:

We are each called to lay down our lives in small ways each day so that other people can be raised up in some way.

Personal Reflection:

Watch today's BLE video (BestLentEver.com/Day25) and write down the one thing that resonates most with you.

For whom are you willing to lay down your life?

What is God saying to you today?

Recommended Reading:

Rediscover the Saints
 • Chapter 17

Today's Gospel:
 • Luke 1:26-38

DAY 26 | MOTHER TERESA: TRUTH, BEAUTY, AND GOODNESS

Today's Focus:

A life that lacks truth, beauty, and goodness will ultimately become boring.

Personal Reflection:

Watch today's BLE video (BestLentEver.com/Day26) and write down the one thing that resonates most with you.

_____

_____

_____

_____

_____

_____

How do you celebrate truth, beauty, and goodness?

_____

_____

_____

_____

_____

_____

What is God saying to you today?

Recommended Reading:

Rediscover the Saints
  • Chapter 18
Today's Gospel:
  • John 5:31–47

DAY 27 | STAFF REFLECTION

Today's Focus:
Amazing Possibilities

Personal Reflection:
Watch today's BLE video (BestLentEver.com/Day27) and write down the one thing that resonates most with you.

_____

_____

_____

_____

_____

_____

_____

How has God opened your heart and mind to new possibilities this week?

_____

_____

_____

_____

_____

_____

_____

What is God saying to you today?

Recommended Reading:

Today's Gospel:
• John 7:1-2, 10, 25-30

DAY 28 | GOSPEL REFLECTION: LAZARUS

Today's Focus:

Today's Gospel is about resurrection. By raising Lazarus from the dead, Jesus demonstrates his power over life and death and foretells his Resurrection.

Personal Reflection:

Watch today's BLE video (BestLentEver.com/Day28) and write down the one thing that resonates most with you.

What aspect of your life do you need Jesus to raise from the dead?

What is God saying to you today?

"I am the resurrection and the life; whoever believes in me, even if he dies, will live, and everyone who lives and believes in me will never die."

John 11:25

Recommended Reading:

Tomorrow's Gospel:
  • John 11:1-45

FIFTH SUNDAY OF LENT I WEEK IN REVIEW

Today's Focus:

A Week in Review

Personal Reflection:

Watch today's BLE video (BestLentEver.com/FifthSunday) and write down the one thing that resonates most with you.

_____

_____

_____

_____

_____

_____

_____

Looking back on this week, what have you learned about yourself, God, and the world that you hope will change the way you live next week?

_____

_____

_____

_____

_____

_____

What is God saying to you today?

Recommended Reading:

Rediscover the Saints
  • Chapters 15 - 18

DAY 29 | MARY MACKILLOP: AUSTRALIA'S FIRST SAINT

Today's Focus:

Champions love coaching. They love to be corrected, because they know it will make them better. This is true in sports, business, relationships, and spirituality. It is true in every area of life.

Personal Reflection:

Watch today's BLE video (BestLentEver.com/Day29) and write down the one thing that resonates most with you.

How coachable are you?

What is God saying to you today?

"The people of your place and time need more holy moments to inspire them to discover their own capacity for goodness."

Matthew Kelly,
Rediscover the Saints

Recommended Reading:

Rediscover the Saints
• Chapter 19

Today's Gospel:
• John 8:1-11

DAY 30 | ANTHONY OF THE DESERT: BE BOLD

Today's Focus:

When you decide to walk with God, you will have to make tough choices, courageous decisions.

Personal Reflection:

Watch today's BLE video (BestLentEver.com/Day30) and write down the one thing that resonates most with you.

_____

_____

_____

_____

_____

Is the culture helping you or hurting you?

_____

_____

_____

_____

_____

_____

_____

What is God saying to you today?

Recommended Reading:

Rediscover the Saints
  • Chapter 20

Today's Gospel:
  • John 8:21–30

DAY 31 | NICHOLAS: HOLDING CHRISTMAS IN YOUR HEART

Today's Focus:

There is something about the spirit of Christmas that brings out the best in people.

Personal Reflection:

Watch today's BLE video (BestLentEver.com/Day31) and write down the one thing that resonates most with you.

_____

_____

_____

_____

_____

_____

What can you learn from the real Santa?

_____

_____

_____

_____

_____

_____

What is God saying to you today?

"Jesus' concern form people's physical and material needs is one of the things that set him apart from the spiritual leaders of his time. He wasn't just interested in the spiritual well-being of people; he was interested in the whole person."

Matthew Kelly,
Rediscover the Saints

Recommended Reading:

Rediscover the Saints
  • Chapter 21
Today's Gospel:
  • John 8:31-42

DAY 32 | MARY: BEAUTIFUL SURRENDER

Today's Focus:

The saints did things wholeheartedly.

Personal Reflection:

Watch today's BLE video (BestLentEver.com/Day32) and write down the one thing that resonates most with you.

_____

_____

_____

_____

_____

_____

_____

What prevents you from surrendering yourself completely to God?

_____

_____

_____

_____

_____

_____

_____

What is God saying to you today?

"Life is choices. We are constantly making decisions, and the decisions we make today determine who we become tomorrow."

Matthew Kelly,
Rediscover the Saints

Recommended Reading:

Rediscover the Saints
• Chapter 22

Today's Gospel:
• John 8:51-59

DAY 33 | STAFF REFLECTION

Today's Focus:

Amazing Possibilites

Personal Reflection:

Watch today's BLE video (BestLentEver.com/Day33) and write down the one thing that resonates most with you.

_____

_____

_____

_____

_____

_____

How has God opened your heart and mind to new possibilities this week?

_____

_____

_____

_____

_____

_____

What is God saying to you today?

Recommended Reading:

Today's Gospel:
• John 10:31-42

DAY 34 | GOSPEL REFLECTION: HIGHS AND LOWS

Today's Focus:

We have all witnessed or experienced life turning from triumph to tragedy. In tomorrow's Gospel, Jesus equally embraces these deeply human realities.

Personal Reflection:

Watch today's BLE video (BestLentEver.com/Day34) and write down the one thing that resonates most with you.

_____

_____

_____

_____

_____

Describe a time in your life when you experienced triumph and tragedy. How did this affect you spiritually?

_____

_____

_____

_____

_____

What is God saying to you today?

"The earth quaked, rocks were split, tombs were opened, and the bodies of many saints who had fallen asleep were raised."

Matthew 27:52

Recommended Reading:

Tomorrow's Gospel:
• Matthew 26:14-27:66

PALM SUNDAY | WEEK IN REVIEW

Today's Focus:
Hot and Cold

Personal Reflection:
Watch today's BLE video (BestLentEver.com/SixthSunday) and write down the one thing that resonates most with you.

_____

_____

_____

_____

_____

_____

_____

Today, the crowds cheer Jesus, but next week they stand by and watch him get crucified. Are you hot, cold, or lukewarm in your spiritual life right now? Why?

_____

_____

_____

_____

_____

_____

What is God saying to you today?

Recommended Reading:

Rediscover the Saints
• Chapters 19 - 22

DAY 35 | RALPH: LOVE OF LEARNING

Today's Focus:

Continuous learning plays a very important role in reminding us to be patient with ourselves and helping us grow in new and exciting ways spiritually.

Personal Reflection:

Watch today's BLE video (BestLentEver.com/Day35) and write down the one thing that resonates most with you.

_____

_____

_____

_____

_____

_____

What stimulates your curiosity and desire to learn?

_____

_____

_____

_____

_____

_____

What is God saying to you today?

Recommended Reading:

Rediscover the Saints
• Chapter 23

Today's Gospel:
• John 12:1–11

DAY 36 | JAMES: DO NOT BE AFRAID

Today's Focus:

Pilgrimages create a powerful connection between God and his people. They banish our fears and fill us with the courage we need to live the life we were born to live.

Personal Reflection:

Watch today's BLE video (BestLentEver.com/Day36) and write down the one thing that resonates most with you.

How often do you forget that we are just passing through this place?

What is God saying to you today?

Recommended Reading:

Rediscover the Saints
  • Chapter 24

Today's Gospel:
  • John 13:21–33, 36–38

DAY 37 | ALL SAINTS: NOW IS YOUR TIME

Today's Focus:

People don't do anything until they are inspired, but once they are inspired there is almost nothing they can't do.

Personal Reflection:

Watch today's BLE video (BestLentEver.com/Day37) and write down the one thing that resonates most with you.

_____

_____

_____

_____

_____

_____

How can you recapture the wonder of childhood?

_____

_____

_____

_____

_____

_____

_____

What is God saying to you today?

Recommended Reading:

Rediscover the Saints
  • Chapter 25

Today's Gospel:
  • Matthew 26:14–25

HOLY THURSDAY | BREAKING BREAD

Today's Focus:
Sacred Meals

Personal Reflection:
Watch today's BLE video (BestLentEver.com/HolyThursday) and write down the one thing that resonates most with you.

Who do you feel called to break bread with? Perhaps someone you haven't seen in a long time or someone you would like to thank for the contribution they made to your life.

What is God saying to you today?

"If I, therefore, the master and teacher, have washed your feet, you ought to wash one another's feet."

John 13:14

Recommended Reading:

Today's Gospel:
• John 13:1-15

GOOD FRIDAY | UNEXPECTED BEGINNINGS

Today's Focus:

Amazing Possibilities

Personal Reflection:

Watch today's BLE video (BestLentEver.com/GoodFriday) and write down the one thing that resonates most with you.

How has God opened your heart and mind to new possibilities this week?

What is God saying to you today?

"You say I am a king. For this I was born and for this I came into the world, to testify to the truth. Everyone who belongs to the truth listens to my voice."

John 18:37

Recommended Reading:

Today's Gospel:
• John 18:1–19:42

HOLY SATURDAY | GOSPEL REFLECTION: SUNRISE

Today's Focus:

From the very first rays of light at dawn, Jesus fills the world with hope.

Personal Reflection:

Watch today's BLE video (BestLentEver.com/HolySaturday) and write down the one thing that resonates most with you.

_____

_____

_____

_____

_____

_____

What are you most hopeful about at this time in your life?

_____

_____

_____

_____

_____

_____

What is God saying to you today?

Recommended Reading:

Today's Gospel:
• Matthew 28:1-10

EASTER SUNDAY | LIKE NO OTHER

Today's Focus:

Sunday mornings are amazing. They focus our days, weeks, lives, relationships . . . and there has never been a Sunday morning like that Sunday morning.

Personal Reflection:

Watch today's BLE video (BestLentEver.com/EasterSunday) and write down the one thing that resonates most with you.

What part of your life needs resurrection?

What is God saying to you today?

Recommended Reading:

Today's Gospel:
• John 20:1–9

EASTER MONDAY I OUR JOURNEY TO EASTER

Today's Focus:

God feeds us so that we can feed others.

Personal Reflection:

Watch today's BLE video (BestLentEver.com/EasterMonday) and write down the one thing that resonates most with you.

_____

_____

_____

_____

_____

_____

_____

How has this Lenten journey been unique and special for you this year?

_____

_____

_____

_____

_____

_____

What is God saying to you today?

Recommended Reading:

Today's Gospel:
• Matthew 28:8-15

CONCLUSION

Happy, happy Easter! We hope this journey to the Resurrection has been life-giving and resulted in a personal resurrection for you, too.

The good news is this is just the beginning. There are innumerable Holy Moments awaiting you. You have a mission—becoming the-best-version-of-yourself. We hope you accept it, and we hope you'll let us continue to walk with you in this wondrous journey.

For more world-class resources on the Catholic faith and becoming the-best-version-of-yourself, visit DynamicCatholic.com.

May God bless you and all those you love,

The Dynamic Catholic Team

How many people do you know who could benefit from reading this book?

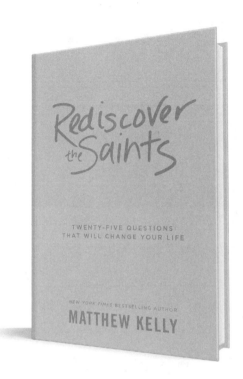

Buy one for yourself, and we will give you a free copy to share with someone you love.

Visit **DynamicCatholic.com/RTS**,
and use the coupon code **RTSBOGO**

NOTES

NOTES

NOTES

NOTES

NOTES

NOTES

NOTES

NOTES

HAVE YOU EVER WONDERED HOW THE CATHOLIC FAITH COULD HELP YOU LIVE BETTER?

How it could help you find more *joy* at work, *manage* your personal finances, *improve* your marriage, or make you a *better* parent?

THERE IS GENIUS IN CATHOLICISM.

When *Catholicism* is lived as it is intended to be, it elevates every part of our lives. It may sound simple, but they say *genius is taking something complex and making it simple.*

Dynamic Catholic started with a dream: to help ordinary people discover the *genius of Catholicism.*

Wherever you are in your journey, we want to meet you there and walk with you, *step by step*, helping you to discover God and become *the-best-version-of-yourself.*

To find more helpful resources, visit us online at DynamicCatholic.com.

 **Dynamic Catholic**

FEED YOUR SOUL.